SCIENCE CORNER

Popcorn

Air

Alice Harman

WAYLAND

Explore the world with **Popcorn** - your complete first non-fiction library.

Look out for more titles in the Popcorn range. All books have the same format of simple text and striking images. Text is carefully matched to the pictures to help readers to identify and understand key vocabulary. www.waylandbooks.co.uk/popcorn

First published in 2013 by Wayland
Copyright © Wayland 2013

Wayland
Hachette Children's Books
338 Euston Road
London NW1 3BH

Wayland Australia
Level 17/207 Kent Street
Sydney NSW 2000

 Produced for Wayland by
White-Thomson Publishing Ltd
www.wtpub.co.uk
+44 (0)843 208 7460

Editor: Alice Harman
Designer: Clare Nicholas
Picture researcher: Alice Harman
Series consultant: Kate Ruttle
Design concept: Paul Cherrill

British Library Cataloguing in Publication Data
Harman, Alice.
   Air. -- (Science corner)(Popcorn)
   1. Air--Juvenile literature.
   I. Title II. Series
   551.5-dc23

   ISBN: 978 0 7502 7762 4

Wayland is a division of Hachette Children's Books,
an Hachette UK company.
www.hachette.co.uk

Printed and bound in China

Picture/illustration credits:
Peter Bull 23; Stefan Chabluk 5, 8, 12; Corbis: Richard T. Nowitz 17; Dreamstime: Fiona Deaton 21; Robert Harding: Andrew McConnell 14; Shutterstock: pirita 4, oliveromg 6, 7t Sheri Armstrong, 7b David Ashley, 9 Apollofoto, 10 Space Factory, 11 Krzysztof Wiktor, Kotenko Oleksander 13, Melissa Brandes 15, Steve Bower 16, 16 inset Carlos Caetano, elwynn 18, Mark William Richardson 19, Cbenjasuwan 21, See-Now 21; Wikimedia: Anke Hueper 20.

Every effort has been made to clear copyright. Should there be any inadvertent omission, please apply to the publisher for rectification.

 Contents

 What is air?

Air is all around us, but we cannot see it. We can feel air when it moves, such as when the wind blows.

The wind makes kites fly up in the sky.

Air is a mixture of gases. The main gases are nitrogen, oxygen and carbon dioxide. Air also contains water, in a gas called water vapour.

This diagram shows how much of each gas is in air.

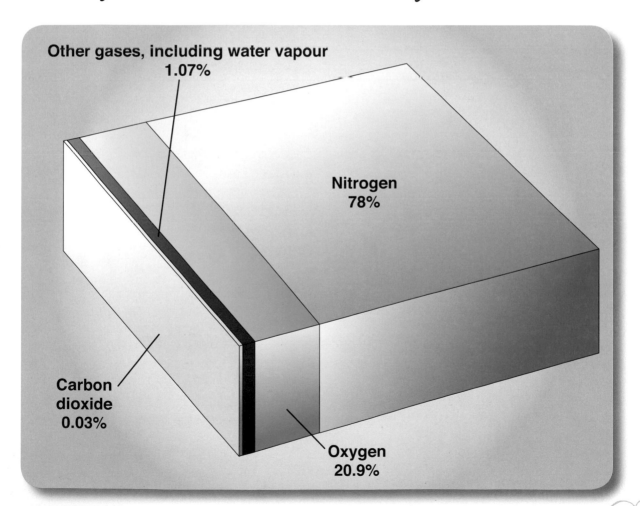

Other gases, including water vapour
1.07%

Nitrogen
78%

Carbon
dioxide
0.03%

Oxygen
20.9%

Air and animals

Almost all animals, including humans, need oxygen to stay alive. We get this oxygen by breathing air into our bodies.

Oxygen gives energy to people and other animals.

Animals that live in water also need oxygen. Some take in oxygen from the water around them. Others come up to breathe air above water.

▶ Fish take in oxygen from the water around them.

▼ Whales breathe oxygen from the air, like people do.

Some whales only come up to breathe every two hours!

Breathing air

When we breathe, we pull air into our bodies and then push it back out. We use our lungs to do this.

You breathe up to 30,000 times a day!

Our lungs fill with air as we breathe in. They empty as we breathe out.

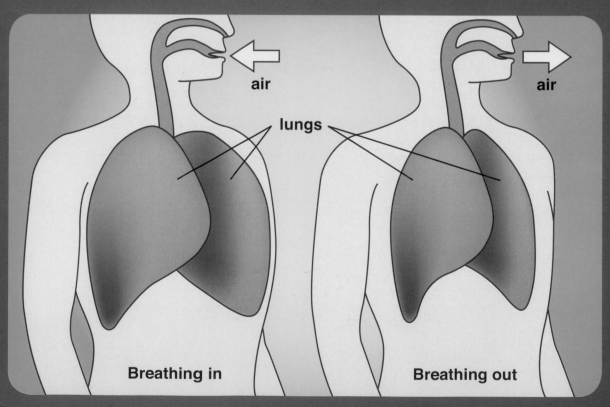

air

lungs

air

Breathing in

Breathing out

Most people can breathe without having to think about it. When you sleep, your body keeps breathing.

When we want to blow out a candle, we can take in a big breath and push the air out quickly!

 Air and plants

Plants need carbon dioxide, not oxygen, for energy. They take in carbon dioxide from the air and give out oxygen.

Plants have tiny holes in their leaves. Air flows into and out of the plant through them.

Large trees take in lots of carbon dioxide. If we didn't have any trees, there would be too much carbon dioxide in the air.

Giant redwood trees are some of the tallest trees in the world.

11

Water in the air

Water vapour in the air comes
from water in the land and ocean.
The sun heats the water and it
turns into water vapour.

Water vapour rises up through the air. It is invisible.

The air high above the ground is very cold. When water vapour rises very high, it gets cold and turns into water again. The water forms clouds.

Water comes down from the clouds as rain or snow.

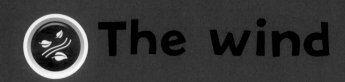 The wind

The wind is invisible, but it can move visible
things. Sandstorms happen when
the wind passes over a desert
and carries the sand along.

Sandstorms
can be as tall
as 850 people
standing on
top of each
other!

This sandstorm is moving towards
a village in Eritrea, in East Africa.

The wind can move very fast and be very strong. It can cause lots of damage. People can be hurt by objects moved by the wind.

Storms with very fast winds can break apart trees and tear down houses.

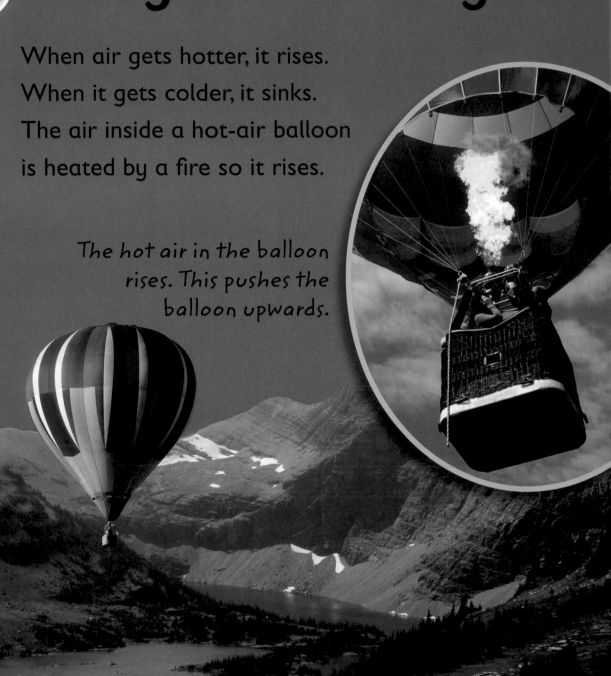

Rising and sinking air

When air gets hotter, it rises.
When it gets colder, it sinks.
The air inside a hot-air balloon
is heated by a fire so it rises.

The hot air in the balloon
rises. This pushes the
balloon upwards.

When there is a fire inside a building, the hot air and smoke rises up to the ceiling. Down on the floor, the air is cooler and clearer.

When there is a fire, it is better to crawl on the floor than to walk or run.

Fire drills help us practise what to do if there is a fire.

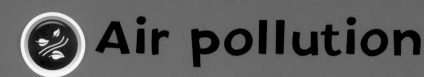Air pollution

Breathing clean air keeps our bodies healthy. Sometimes, there are gases in the air that are unhealthy for us to breathe. This is called air pollution.

Cars cause lots of air pollution in cities.

Burning fuel such as coal and gas produces air pollution. It gives out lots of carbon dioxide, which is also bad for the environment.

Smoke from factories and power stations pollutes the air.

 Wind power

Wind farms use the wind to move
big machines called wind turbines.
This gives energy that we can use
for electricity.

Many wind farms are built in the ocean.
The wind here can be very strong.

People can put a small wind turbine in their garden or on their roof. This provides free electricity for their house.

Wind power is good for the environment because it doesn't cause pollution.

What does it mean?

Try to match up the words on the left side with the correct meaning. You can read back through the book to find the answer if you can't remember it.

1. wind turbine

2. carbon dioxide

3. air pollution

4. oxygen

5. lungs

6. water vapour

A. gas in the air that plants need to stay alive

B. gas that cools high in the sky and forms clouds

C. gas in the air that animals need to stay alive

D. part of the body that we use for breathing air

E. machine that is moved by wind, and gives energy that we can use for electricity

F. unhealthy and unsafe materials, such as poison gases, in the air

Make a wind spinner

You can make a wind spinner that will spin around in the wind.

You will need:
paper plate · black pen
· colouring pens
· scissors · hole punch
· string

1. On the paper plate, use the black pen to draw a spiral shape from the centre outwards. Use the colouring pens to decorate the plate.

2. Ask an adult to help you carefully cut out the spiral along the black line.

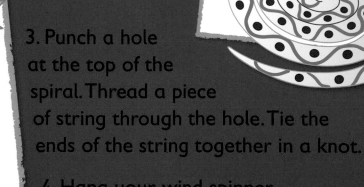

3. Punch a hole at the top of the spiral. Thread a piece of string through the hole. Tie the ends of the string together in a knot.

4. Hang your wind spinner somewhere outside, where it can move in the wind. Try hanging it on a tree branch.

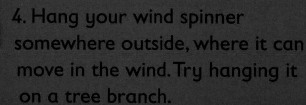

23

Glossary

candle stick of wax with a piece of cotton running through it

coal hard, dark substance that is found underground and burned as fuel

desert large area of dry, sandy ground with very little water

electricity power that makes lightbulbs, televisions, computers and many other things work

environment natural world

gas form of material that is not solid or liquid

fuel material that gives out energy or power

invisible something that we can't see with our eyes

oil greasy liquid that burns well and is used to power cars

poison substance that can hurt or kill a living thing

storm type of weather with lots of wind and rain or snow

visible something that we can see with our eyes

water vapour when water gets very hot, it turns from a liquid into a gas called water vapour

Index

EXPLORE THE WORLD WITH THE POPCORN NON-FICTION LIBRARY!

- Develops children's knowledge and understanding of the world by covering a wide range of topics in a fun, colourful and engaging way
- Simple sentence structure builds readers' confidence
- Text checked by an experienced literacy consultant and primary deputy-head teacher
- Closely matched pictures and text enable children to decode words
- Includes a cross-curricular activity in the back of each book

WATCH OUT! **Near Water** — Honor Head

HISTORY CORNER **The Great Fire of London** — Jenny Powell

SCIENCE CORNER **Sound and Hearing** — Angela Royston

FAMILIES **My Mum** — Katie Dicker

GOOD FOOD **Vegetables** — Julia Adams

PEOPLE WHO HELP US **Police** — Honor Head

PEOPLE WHO HELP US **Firefighters** — Honor Head

GEOGRAPHY CORNER **Rainforests** — Ruth Thomson

A YEAR OF FESTIVALS **Muslim Festivals** — Honor Head

HISTORY CORNER **The Gunpowder Plot** — Jenny Powell

IN SPACE **Planets** — Chris Oxlade

SEASONS **Winter** — Kay Barnham

FREE DOWNLOADS!

Countries: Teachers' Notes

Countries: Spain

OVER 50 TITLES TO CHOOSE FROM!

- Written by an experienced teacher
- Learning objectives clearly marked
- Provides information on where the books fit into the curriculum
- Photocopiable so pupils can take them home

www.waylandbooks.co.uk/downloads